So what?

By Femi Ajayi

Published by New Generation Publishing in 2020

First Edition

ISBN: 978-1-80031-977-6

www.newgeneration-publishing.com

New Generation Publishing

I would like to dedicate this book to God almighty Himself, He is the inspiration behind this book. I would like to appreciate my family for their support all through the years and I would also like to express my gratitude to my wife Benny for believing so much in me.

Contents

Introduction

The understanding of success cannot be overemphasized. Over the years, scholars, academicians, philosophers have tried to explain this ever-important subject to us; sadly, the deeper truths have never been unveiled until now. This book is a revelation to what was unknown. The diction is such that, you don't need a dictionary to decode it. It is simple yet effective. You have read books, this one as you will find is different. By taking time to read and study this book, you are half way towards the actualization your aspiration. I applaud you in advance.

Small Beginnings

Our lives are constantly monitored and sometimes scrutinized by people, whom we often try to impress. Our self-worth is measured solely on their approval and acceptance. When we get the slightest acknowledgement, we feel accepted. This need for acceptance is the reason for the many vices we see today.

Ironically, people who achieve a lot are not driven by public opinion. In truth, the people's favourite eventually become major failures because they were not self-driven to achieve their cause in the first place.

Elon Musk is today a name of a great influence, but that was not always the case. There was a time no one knew him, there was a time he had nothing but his ideas to his name.

Tiger Woods suffered a major setback in his career. The former number one golf player in the world became nothing more than a joke; news presenters called him names; sports analysists told to him to quit.

He survived a messy divorce, had a mental break down, you name it, Tiger Woods saw it all. But he didn't forget what his strength was. He kept at it; they laughed but he continued practising, day and night. No wonder he beat all the odds and eventually won the Masterclass. Miracles do still happen, even today.

The craving for public attention has driven so many people into a new level of mediocrity; individuals doing absurd and insane things to gain a useless popularity which often doesn't translate to huge financial gains.

People will be people regardless. We are humans; yes, we have similarities, however, we are not the same. When I say that, I mean we are different in our ideas, thoughts and perception of the world. This singular difference is why some people fail, while others succeed.

The very fact that we all breathe in the same air; have the same allocated hours and have blood run through our veins says a lot. The excuses we give to our lack of achievements may in fact be nothing short of a lie.

The world is not exactly a friendly place, that is no more a secret, but there are people who have thrived and excelled through it all. Men and women born in extreme poverty who rose to control major enterprises and global organisations in the world today.

See Right

Success or failure is ultimately personal; it is not circumstantial, hereditary or sheer luck as a lot of people think. It is deliberate, calculated and intentional. Now don't get me wrong, you may be in a situation right now and think, "I didn't plan for this".

I have been there. It's a phase in your life; it doesn't have to become you. The odds may not look good, but the miracle only begins if you choose to see things from the right perspective.

Nick Vujicic was born without limbs. He struggled at the beginning of his life. The pains he bore were simply unimaginable. The future looked bleak. He had the perfect alibi to be a nobody. But we all know now that this is not the case.

Not only is he a prolific world-acclaimed writer, he is also a motivational speaker with a difference. He is a living proof of God's omnipotence. The question you need to ask yourself now is: If a limbless man can make so much difference, what are you WAITING FOR?

It is never about the circumstance you find yourself; it is mostly about how you see it and what you do about it. For with every challenge comes within it the solution to resolve it. It is a mystery that only a few can understand.

I don't condone racism. I believe a lot of racist people are ignorant and knowledge deprived. However, if you let the world or society determine your worth based on your colour, race or ethnicity, you have by your own hand marred your future.

The importance of this is crucial; understanding your worth and value will boost your self-esteem. This ultimately forms our confidence and general morale. "As a man thinks in his heart so is, he" Proverbs 23vs 7.

In your journey to success, you will encounter “unfriendly waters”, however the muddiest looking mud may have a very potent cleaning power. Sometimes it’s not what we see but how we see that counts.

Today I visited the Naval Base Park here in Perth, Western Australia. It was not a smooth walk to say the least, the path was very steep and I almost fell down a couple of times. There I was about a thousand feet above the ground, the view was breathe-taking.

The rigor and the pain for climbing was gone; I knew if I had the chance to do it again, I wouldn’t think twice. The problem is not whether or not we want a change; the problem is choosing to ignore the beauty that change would bring. So, you tell yourself it’s not worth it, let’s keep it safe. Let’s do absolutely nothing.

And who can blame you, it’s not like you are competing with anyone. A lot of people are living a life that is classified as comfortable. No high ambitions, just generally living. Hence, no drive for any major change.

I worked once in a manufacturing firm in Lagos, Nigeria. After two years of hard and exemplary work, I had an urge by the holy spirit to leave. Now, I didn’t have any other job at that time and getting one wasn’t exactly a walk in the park.

For days I contemplated my next move. Once again I felt led to become a teacher. You see, this actually does bring some not so good memories. I remember days that I would hop from one school to the other on a motor bike carrier called “Okada”.

I was zealous and ready; failure was never an option. I remember visiting an uncle of mine one time and when our conversation headed to towards what I did for a living, he almost fell off the chair from laughter. He must have thought I was a joke. In Africa, teachers are considered the least in food-chain. They are mostly highly disregarded and under-valued. Most teachers cannot get by on their salaries. However, I decided to do things quite differently.

I started out teaching one school, then through referrals, they became five, one school each day of the week. Before long, I had a training centre at my grandma's house, where I taught both old and young computer appreciation.

I didn't have a car, but I was better off than when I was a branch manager of the manufacturing firm I worked with. I had become my own boss in a way. I was in charge of my future and destiny.

Our journey is very crucial, don't deny your small beginnings. It is often a stage, a place of isolation; it's a place of rejection and denial. But it is also a place of birthing, creativity and innovation. A man once said: "When I close my eyes I see".

When we understand just how personal life is, the less we would chase after shadows. The shadows of validation and approval of people who barely know of our existence. It would then become very clear; that at the end of it all, we will find that it is worthless trying to prove a point to anyone.

Success is deliberate. It is very intentional. That means you have to be unapologetic when working towards achieving your goals. Usually the obstacles that I find mostly potent are the human factor. The close relations, who know you well; they will give you very valid reason why you are meant to fail.

I have heard people say, "don't say how you got there, just get there". I strongly disagree. The making of a star is an intricate part of his life that should not be ignored. Sometimes, stars are born… often times, they are made.

You may very well say, you are not where you want to be, rejoice because you are somewhere. Right there is a story waiting to be told. And in writing and creating your story, age is irrelevant. As they say it's just a number. What's most crucial is recognising that you truly have something someone needs to hear.

You Have Nothing to Prove

So what? What if it was unpleasant? What if you were hurt? I know this sounds heartless but don't let your previous pain and life mar the glorious future ahead of you. Story might just very well be what someone was waiting all his life to hear. Your experience may very well be the elixir to steer a generation, even unborn, in the right direction. You are alive, there is hope.

The challenge with people today, is they have a lot to prove to people. This singular flaw is the reason for so much penury, even in seemingly rich societies or countries. They choose to live a life of mediocrity just as long as they are able to hide their true circumstance.

You will come across people who will tell why you are not good enough. Why they think you won't excel. However, this is where your true resilience is tested. Why is this important? The strength of a solder is only known in battle.

Criticism often breed greatness, when done right. It may not often times appear that way but, people who criticize others forget themselves in the process, resulting to little or no self-improvement at all on their part.

Have you ever seen or met any food critic who owns a restaurant? Hardly. This is not surprising, I know about constructive criticisms, thank God for them, however; no criticism stays "constructive" for long.

Successful people have what we call 'a thick skin'. They don't necessary always look like what they have been through. It may sound like something from a horror movie, but it's a fact that keeps a lot of people moving, regardless of whatever hurdle life throws at them.

Even when your eyes are wide open, they have to be shut and blind to certain distractions in life. The need for self-gratification and public approval, especially in an age where social media is the determinant of a good life.

People who have something to prove usually end up proving absolutely nothing… Never find yourself desperate to show anyone your creed or status – it is a waste of creativity.

I live in one of the most prosperous countries in the world. It is such a blessing to call Australia home. The history of Australia is one forged from love, resilience and forgiveness. One major attribute you will instantly recognise is that Australians are givers.

The journey of success and what it is births something far more within us, for those who want to succeed continuously; one thing that you will find very useful is putting others first.

Selfish people never really accomplish much and whatever little they do is quickly forgotten.

Part of my job description is mentoring young people. A few days ago, while coming from Hungry Jacks with my mentee, a lady approached me. She seemed quite unkempt and untidy. My first instinct was to walk away, but I didn't.

"I am hungry," she said, looking at my meal. Without a second thought, I gave her almost half of my meal. She was stunned as we walked away. I could still hear her say "thank you so much, mate!"

The young man with me was even more shocked and he offered to share some of his meal with me. He later on said he had never seen anything like that ever before, where someone could share his meal with a total stranger.

The true meaning of success is printed in the number of lives we change. Success is influencing the world to aspire to your aspiration, and since most aspirations are good, it is safe to say success is indeed leaving someone better than you meet them.

Our lord and saviour Jesus Christ is an epitome of success by all means. He invested himself, his time and resource in people. He provided for his followers, stood with them when things were tough and ultimately died for them.

His thirty-three years life was mostly people-centred. Not much can be said of the things he did for His family or Himself. He wasn't propelled by riches or fame, He just simply wanted to affect the lives of people around Him positively and He did!

Stevland Hardaway Morris A.K.A Stevie Wonder was born blind. He had a perfect excuse to be a nobody and like most people would be in his situation and live a life of absolute defeat, but he chose to refuse to let his disability stop him from becoming the person whose music we can't get a enough of.

Every situation we find ourselves has two potentials, firstly to destroy us (if we let it), otherwise if could be the sole reason why we become a symbol of hope for a generation that so desperately needs some.

I knew a man once, he had been in prison for so many years. He had taken all kind of drugs but at some point, his life was totally transformed. It didn't stop there, he now helps people around him fight drug addiction through his rehab program.

A lot of times, failure is always misinterpreted. You have not failed simply because your plan didn't work. However, if you choose to stop trying on account of your inability to bring your plan into fruition? Then yes, you have failed.

I know you may have heard something similar to this before, but it is very true. Consider this: planting a tree often requires a lot of years of nurturing, attention and dedication.

You can't just put the seed in the soil and leave it there. No, it's got to be a constant and frequent care. Even with when all this is done, there are no certainty that the tree will turn out well.

Your failures may actually be just a moment of stagnation, it should not categorically define the outcome of your life. You alone have the power to push yourself out of your current state.

There is absolutely nothing in this world that has a big enough power to stop you... Do you think you are too old to dream? Colonel Sanders didn't start till he was sixty. Today, even after his death, Kentucky Fried Chicken is one of the most established fast food-chains today.

Perhaps you have a terminal illness, whose report would you believe? Doctors are awesome and brilliant, but guess what, they are not God! I know this is where some of you are going shake your head.

The only final report you must believe is the divine one. I know it's not fashionable these days to talk and sound like this, but it is absolutely true. I have enjoyed supernatural health for over a decade.

I don't take any form of medicine; I have relied solely on my faith in God and so far, He hasn't disappointed me. Now am I saying don't take medications? No, that's not my point. My point is even if your doctor has said you are done, there is a chance that God has another opinion. So, make sure you hear from God before you pack your bags.

Life is beautiful indeed, however what makes it worth living and beautiful is not far from our perspective of life.

What Do You Want

> "The first principle of success is desire – knowing what you want. Desire is the planting of your seed"
>
> – Robert Collier

What do you want? Seems like a simple question, right? It's not an answer we all have, unfortunately.

If you do not know what you want, how would you know what to do to get it? Furthermore, how would you even know when you have it. Having a definite and precise picture of your dream is as important as actualizing it?

A farmer plants a seed of the harvests he wants, he has a picture in his mind on what he will gathering at a particular season. Also, a skilled farmer; he knows what plants are best for certain times of the year.

The importance of this cannot be overemphasized. Not having a clear perception of your dream and aspiration would ultimately make you complacent and eventually accept whatever life throws at you.

There are doctors who wanted to be disc jockeys, lawyers who should have been farmers. I understand the fact that some factors could be attributed to such circumstances, but I guess the big question would then be: are you happy doing what you do now?

Circumstances would always a play a part in our lives, regardless of what stage you are in life, be assured it's inevitable.

Think of it has as a sail-boat; you must be able to understand how to use the wind to propel the boat.

While it is most certain that the wind will blow, the time and duration is usually unknown, so a good helmsman must know how and when to position the boat to take full advantage of wind for speed in the right direction.

Our view of life's unexpected challenges would ultimately determine the level of our failure or success. People who look at the "cup half full" tends to live a better and longer life.

A prognosis isn't the end of the road. There is life as long as hope exists, it's not just a cliché, it is a reality. Don't pack your bags yet, don't succumb to any news that could potentially take your hope away.

Learn to appreciate the small victories you achieve; it's not just something you do for your kids, it is very helpful for you too as an adult. Little drops of water could very well become a large body of water given the right time and volume.

The Shark Tank is renowned for birthing great start-ups that potentially become business successes which other businesses model after. As such, the "Sharks" analyse the entrepreneurs, evaluate their businesses, their income and expenses etc to determine whether they are worth their investments or not.

There have been businesses considered a high risk that eventually became a global success. Despite the fact that the panel decided they were not worth their investment.

Even in the thickest jungle, there is always an exit route. The end of that road, may just very well be the beginning of another wonderful road.

Have a Plan

"By failing to prepare, you are preparing to fail"

– Anonymous

There is nothing wrong with having a desire, aspiration or dream. However, the problem occurs when dreaming and hoping is all you do.

Everyone wants to be a millionaire; nobody hates money and having a lot of it is even better. While some people hinge their fate on lotteries or gambling (no offence to them) only a few people have decided to actually strategize, and create a solution to meet a human need, thereby creating a steady flow of income.

Always remember that the fact that you want something, or want to be somewhere does not mean it will happen. The fulfilment of any endeavour or goal, is solely dependent on the disciplined planning and time-staking effort an individual put into achieving that dream.

Think about it, you can't just wake up one day and decide you are now a medical doctor or a lawyer or a biochemist; if that's true, it also means you can't be that success you want overnight. It doesn't happen that way.

You must be organised. You must schedule meetings, attend adequate training, and commit to all the activities that would eventually birth your goals into fruition.

I am privileged to mentor some young men here in Perth. One of them just got his driver's license (manual). What makes his story remarkable is the fact that while most people have to fail at least once to pass the test, this young man passed it the very first time!

I couldn't resist asking him how he did it! He did more than the required lessons of seventy hours, he read all the books and watched so many YouTube videos, no wonder he passed so well. And his folks also passed their PDA (Practical Driving Assessment) the very first time too!

This book is a result of planning, setting time aside to research and examine the subjects being discussed carefully. And ensuring that I communicate in a clear and concise manner without any ambiguity.

Think about it this way, before you go on a trip by air, you are given an itinerary which tells you the flight schedules, stop-overs, if any, take off and landings. Have you ever been on a plane without getting one? Or have you ever boarded a flight to Germany and ended up in France?

Life is like that, you have to plan your life journey, how are you going to do it when will it be done? Only those who have appointment to keep know they are early or late; without a plan time becomes a burden rather than a gift.

Do you have a yearly goal? Why not? How then do you measure your progress? What are you missing? What should you do better? The answers are all embedded in your yearly or monthly goals. They will help you to be accountable.

Be focused

> "Lack of direction, not lack of time, is the problem. We all have twenty-four hour days"
>
> – Zig Ziglar

Focus, what really is it? The dictionary defines Focus as the "centre of Interest" or activity as a noun; as a verb it is paying a particular attention to something".

How powerful is focus? Have you ever seen a magnifying glass? I played with once when I was a kid, most people have. You generate an immense power of heat energy by simply focusing the glass on an object with the presence of sunlight. That's it!

When you put everything else aside and concentrate on one single thing, the probability on excelling in that field is more likely than trying to several things at once.

When you visit a Podiatry, his/her objective is helping you with any ailment regarding your FEET! So, if for any reason you are asked about eyes for instance would be quite a surprise.

In this success journey, you will have to understand your strengths and MAGNIFY them. No, it's not insolence, it is an absolute necessity for you to succeed at any endeavour you find yourself during.

Avoid the temptation of checking out what's going on in your "neighbour's kitchen". I don't mean that literally. But mind your business! It sounds a little harsh doesn't it.

There are three kinds of people in this world: people who write the news, people who read the news and people who make the NEWS! The last category of people actually make things happen, they are dedicated and focused enough to attract attention of others.

A lot of people hinge their lives one what a "New Maker" does, I dare say some would ever be jobless without them, but are these people born that way? Well, we have heard of Royals stepping down from royal duties, we have seen celebrities who loathe fame passionately.

But I know of people with no talent, not of royal heritage and most importantly, no money and by themselves have chosen to make their own noise.

Tyler Perry was born in a humble African America family from New Orleans, Louisiana. At a time when the movie and theatre industry underwent a major shake-up, he remained on a path he had forged for himself, writing, producing and directing his own works.

That the world is changing, doesn't always mean you have to. I understand you have to upgrade your skills and develop yourself however, your vision for your destination should not be BLURRY! Know your destination, and let your eyes be fully on the path to reach it.

Don't do it alone

> "Two are better than one, because they have a good return for their labour"
>
> Ecce 4:9

Success CANNOT be achieved in isolation. At some point, you have to work with someone, whether it is a mentor, life coach, family member or even a pastor.

These associations help fast track our growth and maturity enough for a perfect harvest. They are very important. You must understand this road you are on won't be a smooth one, there will be moments you will wish you never started in the first place.

There will be times you just want to give everything up and hand over the reins to someone else. These people will keep you grounded; they will give a sort of anchor during your stormy season.

As such, picking them won't be an easy task. You have to be sure of their dedication and genuine interest towards you, your dreams and aspiration. Once this is certain, then informed them as your make progress; carry them along on every stage you reach.

A read the story of a young man who ran a race and just about a few metres to the finish line, he had a painful muscle pain; he fell down on the tracks screaming in great pain.

A man came to his aid, hopping on one leg; with his right arm around his helper's shoulder, he finished the race. An interview later revealed that man was the athlete's father.

We can do a lot alone but we can go further with the right associations. Having the right people in your circle will also help increase your confidence and self-esteem. Knowing that someone else believes in your vision is invaluable.

Although Hitler's ideology was wrong, he had a large followership that ultimately made him almost unstoppable. He spoke and people listened. Nothing else mattered; they believed in his vision and they planned to ensure it happened.

Alexander the Great was a phenomenon, his victories are still the subject of discuss even today. But that success was mostly attributed to his solders. They were "sold-out" to his plan to conquer the world.

Most success stories are as a result of some sort of "Push" from other people who believe in a dreamer's dream. If you don't think this is important, then I will ask you this why do some people take their own lives? There you go, sadly some kids have done it because they have been bullied at school; adults for different reasons financial, health. Spoken words are efficacious.

Furthermore, when it comes to marriage, while I understand the complexities of sentiment and emotion, it is important that your spouse is on the same "page" as you are.

My wife Benny has been a key pillar in my life, she has been very supportive I couldn't ask for a better helpmate, I am grateful for her. When your spouse has your back your life will be much easier.

However, don't be apologetic. There is absolutely no point in hanging around people that add no value to your life. It's like putting a cog in your own wheels When it comes to succeeding in life, it is alright to be picky with your association, but when you are blessed to have the right people, don't let them GO!

There is always more

The question is not how big your dream is, the real question is how big do you think God is? Our comprehension of the this would further increase our desire to dream even bigger!

For you to know how big He is let's first consider who God is, shall we? Why is this relevant? Well, there has been a lot of debate regarding the existence of a supreme being. There are people who have fought to alienate anything suggesting God or the belief in Him.

It's not new, you know, man has always been in denial, but the facts are there, they will always be. The fact that He cannot be seen further strengthens the atheist's conviction to nullify this truth.

The law of gravity exists, whether we believe it or not; we do not see the air we breathe, yet we cannot do without it. There is nothing more real than the one who made everything.

I know that reading this now you may be tempted to drop this book and say "Here we go again another religious sicko". If you read my profile at the back of this book you will understand that I am not. Well, hopefully.

But in all seriousness, it is just impossible to talk about success without understanding its source. Yes success begins and ends with God Himself. He is the foundation of success.

I have never been a believer in evolution, I will never be. I can't fathom how a sophisticated machine like a human can come from an ANIMAL! The human brain alone a proof that theory is calculated lie.

God made us, and he planned for everyone to succeed and succeed very well. Jeremiah 32 vs 27 says "I am the LORD, the God of all mankind. Is anything too hard for me". A question that only a supernatural being can ask. Compelling the whole of humanity to understand that He is in fact limitless in ability and capability.

However, the most striking and intriguing factor about this great and magnificent God is the fact that he actually wants you to succeed. 3 John 2 says "Beloved, I wish above all things that thou mayest prosper and be in health, even as thy soul prospereth".

If the above scripture is true then it becomes very clear that, apart from being the source of all mankind and the whole of creation, God's ultimate wish and desire is for us to be successful.

That's no shock at all. It's His nature. He programmed everything to run excellently FOREVER! God is that big. So, whenever you are thinking of doing something, or planning on achieving a goal; think mostly outside your human reach.

I know these days it's not quite politically correct to talk like this especially about God, but it doesn't change the truth no one can achieve lasting greatness outside God's help.

Let your expectations be humanly impossible, let it be so big that everyone you tell it to would simply laugh; don't take offence, it is allowed. It's not always about your dream…do you have enough faith to make it a reality.

About two years ago, Benny and I went for a walk, I suddenly told her, "You know, honey, would we would be moving into our own house after this lease ends." She paused and almost laughed.

We lived in a rented apartment in Osbourne Park for three years, had lots of our business ideas that never kicked off. And we didn't really have massive savings too, so physically it was absolutely and totally impossible.

We visited Nairobi, Kenya, some time ago, but by the time we returned, our first house had been fully built. It took only three months! By August that year we moved in. Today we are looking at other potential opportunities in real estate. But it began with a dream. God is more eager for the fruition of your dream than you could ever be. He takes delight in it.

Every big achievement begins with a dream. They may appear foolish and unthinkable, so what if it's crazy? It might just be precisely the kind of dream that gets God's attention. Remember, He loves to make it happen for you. I am living proof. Don't walk this life's journey alone, do it with God. Please read Romans 10:9.

Acknowledgements

I would like to appreciate my wife Benny for all her love and support on this journey. I would also like to thank my family for always believing in my dreams and most importantly, I thank God for His divine insights and wisdom that led to this book.

About me

Mr Ajayi Olufemi Adeola was born in Lagos Nigeria, now lives in Perth, Western Australia. He is a Member of the Australian Society of Authors, also a member of Australian College of Community & Disability Practitioners. He is also a registered welfare worker with the Australian Community Workers Association. He is a songwriter as well, produced his first song "Everything" in 2017. Femi owns www.inkmotivational.com where he writes inspirational articles regularly.

www.ingramcontent.com/pod-product-compliance
Ingram Content Group UK Ltd.
Pitfield, Milton Keynes, MK11 3LW, UK
UKHW042002190726
13854UKWH00005B/2120

9 781800 319776